How to Bui

Written by Is___ ___

Contents

Collins

Somewhere to shelter

Look outside, and imagine that you have to build a shelter, right now. Where would you start? Probably with a quick look around to see which materials are available ...

Could you grab sticks and leafy branches to weave together? How about stones to prop the sticks up, or mud to act as glue? Maybe you could raid the recycling bin for old cardboard and plastic. Or knock a few bricks from a disused building and use them to make something new!

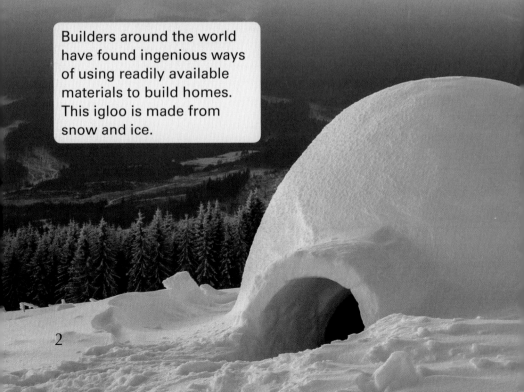

Builders around the world have found ingenious ways of using readily available materials to build homes. This igloo is made from snow and ice.

The way that you use the available materials will depend on the climate you live in, and what you need to shelter from. Do you need materials that trap warmth in, or keep heat out? Do you need to shade yourself from the sun, or protect your possessions from wind and rain?

Builders, architects and engineers must also think about the impact of materials on the environment.

HOUSE HAZARDS!

Look out for these hazards that help builders match materials to climate.

HARD HAT CHALLENGE

Investigate the properties of materials with these hands-on activities.

Organic materials

The oldest homes we know about were made in the Stone Age, more than 14,000 years ago. They were built with materials that were easy to shape using stone tools: branches, leaves, animal skins, and even the bones of a woolly mammoth. These are all **organic** materials.

Mammoths may be extinct, but plant leaves, stems and branches are still popular building materials today. They are easy to find and to use. You don't need heavy machinery to build a family home from bamboo.

palm leaves

Bamboo is a popular building material in Ecuador. These oversized stalks are harder to pull apart than steel, and more difficult to squash than concrete!

light but strong bamboo stalks

Thatch

House builders around the world have developed ways to use the plants that grow locally. Reeds and straw have been used to make thatched roofs for more than 12,000 years. Thatch is a good insulator. It traps air, helping to keep heat inside the house.

Bundles of straw are packed together tightly. They lie at an angle so rainwater runs off before it has a chance to soak in.

5

HOUSE HAZARDS!

Like all things that are alive, or used to be alive, materials made from plants don't last forever. They are attacked by creatures involved in decay, from bacteria and fungi to beetles and woodworms. Lightweight plant materials are also easily damaged by wind and rain and must be repaired or replaced often.

In Stone Age societies, houses weren't expected to last forever. People would move from place to place, building new homes as they went. Lightweight plant materials were perfect.

When people began farming, they wanted to build permanent homes next to their land. They needed tougher materials that lasted longer.

One solution was to use thick logs instead of thin branches. When metal tools were developed, entire tree trunks could be chopped down and stripped of their bark and branches. Thick logs are good insulators, so they became a popular building material in cold areas of the world with large forests.

Log cabins have been built in the same way for hundreds of years.

logs lock together at the joints

Timberrrrrrrrrrrrrrr!

Wood is strong, but also easy to shape into poles and planks, known as timbers. These can be joined together quickly, to build a large, house-shaped frame. In Tudor England, the gaps between the timbers were filled in with wattle and daub or brick.

Today, wood is the most widely used material for home building around the world. It's **renewable** (it really does grow on trees!) and easy to use without special training or expensive tools.

Many timber-framed houses built by the Tudors 500 years ago are still standing today.

wattle and daub

In wet climates, wood-framed houses are covered with a "skin" of brick, stone, concrete or plastic to make them weatherproof. Wood can also be treated to make it resistant to rot, insects and even fire.

More than nine in every ten North American homes have a wooden frame, thanks to the huge forests that cover the continent.

diagonal braces stop the frame wobbling

heavy timbers support roof and floors

Stone materials

More than 120 types of building stone are **quarried** in the UK alone! These rocks are natural materials that formed millions or even billions of years ago.

Heavy machinery cuts and moves stone in a quarry.

no **mortar**

10

Stone is strong under pressure, and isn't easily destroyed by wind or water. These properties make it great for building tough homes, but they also make stone difficult to collect, transport and shape.

It's not surprising that the earliest stone houses were made using whichever stones were found nearby – rubble and small boulders gathered from local river beds, beaches, or landscapes. Dry-stone homes made from local stone are found all around the world. They are made by carefully piling loose stones on top of each other.

stone furniture

The tough stone walls of these 4,000-year-old homes at Skara Brae, Scotland, provided protection from strong winds and driving rain.

For thousands of years, stone was the building material of choice for those who could afford it. Stone is hard-wearing and looks good – there's no need to cover it up with something more weatherproof or attractive. Stone walls are strong enough to bear the weight of a tall building.

The ancient Egyptians developed ways to quarry, move and shape huge blocks of stone, but for hundreds of years cut stone was too expensive for all but the most important buildings. It could only be shaped and placed by skilled **stonemasons**.

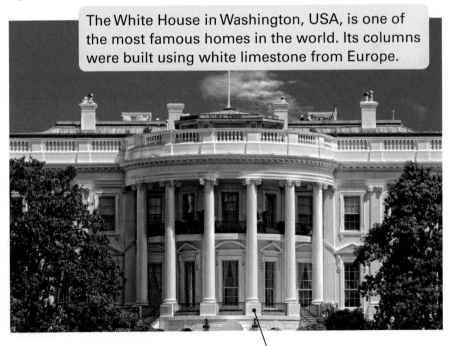

The White House in Washington, USA, is one of the most famous homes in the world. Its columns were built using white limestone from Europe.

tough stone supports
heavy columns

Most houses in Aberdeen, Scotland, were built using local grey granite. The thick stone walls help to control the temperature of a house by trapping heat inside or keeping it out.

no carved details as granite is too hard

HOUSE HAZARDS!

Heavy stone walls that *weren't* built properly could be very dangerous. So many stone walls collapsed in London in the Middle Ages, a law was passed saying they had to be almost a metre thick!

Pick and mix

The properties of stone depend on how the rock originally formed. Rocks such as granite are tough and hard-wearing. Rocks such as sandstone and limestone are softer and easier to shape – though they are more easily damaged by weather. Certain rocks – such as slate and marble – have special properties that make them popular building stones.

HARD HAT CHALLENGE

Collect different types of stone. Compare their hardness by rubbing them against sandpaper. The softest stones will wear away faster, and leave bigger marks.

The end of the "stone age"?

Compared to most other building materials, stone is still difficult and expensive to use. Since the 1800s, human-made building materials such as concrete, brick and metal have replaced many of the old uses of stone. However, the look of stone is still very popular, so builders are finding new ways to use stone for decoration.

Don't be fooled by the rocks – this house is built from inexpensive concrete blocks, covered with a thin layer of stone **cladding**.

Earth materials

The ultimate building material is free, found everywhere, and can be used over and over again. Simply mix earth with water to make … mud!

Mud has been used to build homes for thousands of years. It's soft and sticky when wet, but dries solid. Dried mud is fireproof, and doesn't conduct heat well. This means that a home with mud walls heats up slowly in the sun, and cools down slowly at night. It stays warm in cool climates.

Mud is an eco-friendly building material. People don't have to chop down forests or dig quarries to collect mud. Mud is soft enough to shape by hand, but dries hard in the sun. No wonder mud is one of the most-used building materials on the planet.

Mud has been a popular building material in places near rivers but far from forests. The city of Shibam, in Yemen, was built using mud bricks.

Cob walls

Mixing mud with other materials makes it stronger, tougher and more weatherproof. "Cob" walls are built by mixing mud with sand, small stones and straw or dung. Lumps of the mixture are built up in layers, letting each layer dry before adding the next. Some cob houses are hundreds of years old.

Cob cottages in England are often "whitewashed" with waterproof paint.

thick walls trap heat inside

white paint reflects the sun's heat

Wattle and daub

Wattle and daub homes have been built since the Iron Age, more than 3,000 years ago. Panels woven from wood are "daubed" with a mixture of mud, straw and even animal dung! The wooden wattle makes the walls stronger. The mud daub makes them more weatherproof.

HOUSE HAZARDS!

So what's the dirt on mud? Dried mud swells up when it gets wet, and shrinks in hot, dry weather. All this swelling and shrinking makes the mud crack. Cracked mud walls let in rain, draughts and insects. To overcome these problems, house builders began to turn mud into bricks.

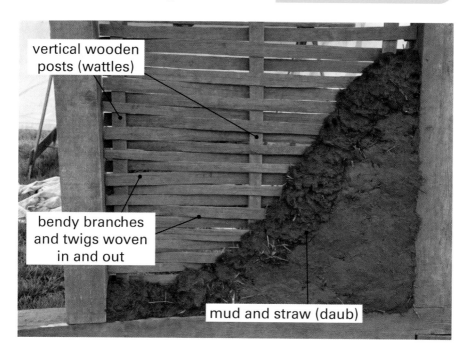

vertical wooden posts (wattles)

bendy branches and twigs woven in and out

mud and straw (daub)

Adobe bricks

Press a sticky mixture of mud, sand and straw into a wooden frame, leave it to dry in the sun and you've made an adobe brick! As the water evaporates, the adobe mixture becomes stiff and hard. The dry bricks can be stacked on top of each other to build walls, and stuck together with wet mud, or tar.

The oldest adobe bricks found are at least 9,500 years old. Most prehistoric wooden or stone homes had a rounded shape, but building with bricks changed the design. Houses became rectangular too.

Adobe walls are strong but easy to build. The mud bricks and the mortar are dried using only the sun's energy, which makes them affordable.

In the Middle East and North Africa, far from large forests, adobe bricks have been a key building material since ancient Egyptian times.

Straw, grass or sticks make the clay brick stronger when it dries.

Clay is the best type of mud for making adobe bricks. It's easy to mould when wet, but hardens as it dries.

A thick adobe wall will take in heat during the day, and releases it slowly at night, helping to keep a house comfortable.

Fired bricks

Heating materials to high temperatures can change their properties. Think about the changes that happen when you bake cake mix.

If clay bricks are heated to high temperatures (900 to 1,200 degrees centigrade), they become much harder and stronger. Bricks **fired** in this way are tougher than many types of stone.

The first fired bricks were made around 5,000 years ago. They became one of the Romans' favourite building materials. Bricks are much easier to build with than stone, and led to new designs.

Some Roman brick buildings are still standing today!

brick

lime mortar

Fired bricks don't crack in the sun like mud, or rot in the rain like reeds, or catch fire like wood.

When the Roman Empire shrank in the 400s, Europeans stopped building with bricks. For hundreds of years, timber, mud bricks and wattle and daub were top of the medieval house builder's shopping list.

While Europeans took a break from bricks, Chinese builders were becoming master bricklayers. Billions of fired bricks were used in the Great Wall of China.

Brick made a comeback in medieval Europe when people began recycling bricks and rubble from Roman buildings to make new homes. From the 1200s, bricks gradually became more popular, especially where no good stone was available. Bricks were easier to build with and could be just as hard-wearing.

At first, bricks were more expensive than natural materials, so they were used sparingly for the new luxury must-have of the time – chimneys!

During the **Industrial Revolution**, brickmakers developed ways to make bricks in factories on a huge scale. This made bricks better and cheaper. In many European countries, brick homes became the norm.

Not just a pretty pattern

Bricks are made in standard sizes, making it easy to lay them in neat rows. Bricks aren't just stacked on top of each other, but are arranged in interlocking patterns. This makes a brick wall much stronger and stops cracks appearing in the mortar.

roof made from
fired clay tiles

patterns
in brickwork

Bricks allowed builders to be creative.
In the 1800s, Dutch bricklayers
developed decorative patterns that
spread to nearby countries.

shaped gable

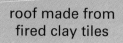

H. DE VRIES

Today, most new homes in
Britain are made of concrete
blocks or a timber frame, with
a thin outer wall of brick.

Cement and concrete

Stone, adobe bricks and clay bricks are stuck together using mortar – a soft mixture that hardens as it dries. At first, mud or tar were the best choices, but around 2,000 years ago, builders came up with a much stronger mortar.

Builders in ancient Greece are thought to have invented cement when they added **lime** (made by heating limestone) to a mixture of sand, water and clay. This made a soft paste that hardened as it dried.

A new recipe

The ancient Romans developed this "artificial stone" into an even stronger material by mixing lime and water with chunks of rock and ash from volcanoes. The mixture was easy to pour or mould into any shape, but set rock-hard as the ingredients reacted together.

This early concrete was so strong, it could be used as a building material itself. It was much quicker and easier to use than real stone. However, the Romans thought concrete looked ugly. They often covered it up with more attractive materials.

concrete

Some Roman concrete buildings, such as Hadrian's Villa, are still standing after more than 2,000 years.

Artificial stone

For hundreds of years, the "natural" concrete invented by the Romans was a builder's best option. Then, from the 1700s, builders started experimenting with different ingredients to develop stronger mortar and concrete.

They perfected the powder known as Portland cement. This is a mixture of many ingredients, including limestone, **shale** and clay, which are crushed up and heated to very high temperatures before being ground into powder. Portland cement is the main ingredient in today's mortar and concrete.

HOUSE HAZARDS!

Concrete sets to form a solid block, like a huge lump of rock. It's good at resisting squeezing forces (high pressure) but cracks if it's twisted or pulled. A plain concrete building can be destroyed if it's shaken by strong winds or an earthquake.

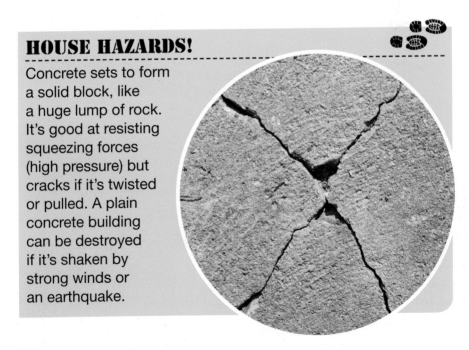

Reinforced concrete

Concrete can be reinforced by combining it with steel. Steel doesn't crack when pulled and twisted, so together the steel and concrete make an unbeatable building material.

Wet concrete is poured over steel rods, which are locked in place as the concrete sets.

concrete

steel rods

Today, you'll find concrete in homes everywhere in the world. It's used in many different forms, from pre-made blocks or panels used to make walls, to wet concrete poured into moulds on site to make foundations, floors and staircases. Like stone, concrete absorbs and loses heat slowly. This means it can help a house to retain heat, or keep heat out.

Concrete blocks

Most of the bricks and blocks used in modern homes are made from concrete rather than clay or stone. Because they are poured rather than carved, concrete bricks can be hollow inside, making them lighter and cheaper. Their large size makes them quick to lay. Concrete blocks aren't as hard-wearing as fired bricks – and don't look as nice – so they are most often used for inner walls and foundations.

Concrete can stand up to heavy loads, so builders can build many storeys on top of concrete foundations.

Creating with concrete

It's easy to mould concrete into unusual shapes, allowing architects to let their imaginations run riot! This is much cheaper than carving shapes from stone.

31

Metal materials

Most metal on Earth is found locked up inside rocks. Metal wasn't widely used for building until people worked out how to extract it in large quantities.

Metals have special properties that make them useful for house building. Unlike stone, brick and concrete, many metals are strong under **tension**. They don't crack or snap easily when forces try to pull them apart. Metals can also be melted and poured, beaten or bent into different shapes.

The Romans used sheets of soft metal, such as bronze and lead, to cover roofs. In the Middle Ages, copper took over as the most popular metal for building. Once a copper roof had been hammered into place, it would stay waterproof for a hundred years or more. However, copper was expensive and only used for the most important buildings and homes.

This copper roof has turned green over time as the metal reacts with the air. This tough outer layer protects the metal underneath, so the roof won't develop leaks.

tile design pressed into the metal

lighter than clay tiles, and easier to lay

Today, sheets of zinc provide a cheaper alternative to copper.

33

The sky's the limit

During the 1700s and 1800s, people began producing iron on a large scale. Iron is a strong metal, so builders began using cast iron beams and columns in the place of brick, stone or timber. In the 20th century, the mass production of steel (a mixture of iron and carbon) led to even more exciting changes to housing.

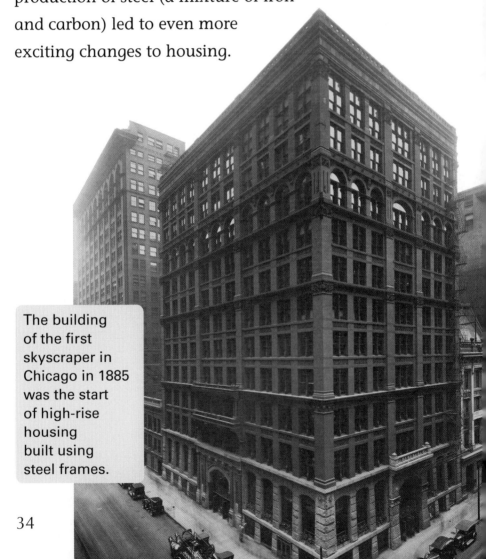

The building of the first skyscraper in Chicago in 1885 was the start of high-rise housing built using steel frames.

Steel beams can span large distances without warping like wood, or cracking like stone. This means that houses can be designed with larger rooms, and walls that don't need to bear a load. Steel-framed homes are popular in parts of the world where wood is attacked by rot or termites.

However, steel is more expensive than wood, and takes much more energy to produce – so it can be damaging to the environment.

This steel frame is so strong that the gaps don't need to be filled in with load-bearing materials. Plastic and glass can be used instead.

Ready-made homes

In the 1900s, other metals and new **alloys** became available to house builders. One of these was aluminium, a strong but very light metal that doesn't rust. In Britain, aluminium was used to build "prefabricated" homes to replace houses that were destroyed during World War Two.

Today, aluminium is found in most homes – in windows, internal walls, gutters, doorframes, conservatories and skylights. Up to 85% of the aluminium used in building today is recycled.

The metal roof and walls of these "prefab" homes were made in a factory, so the finished homes could be put together quickly, like a jigsaw.

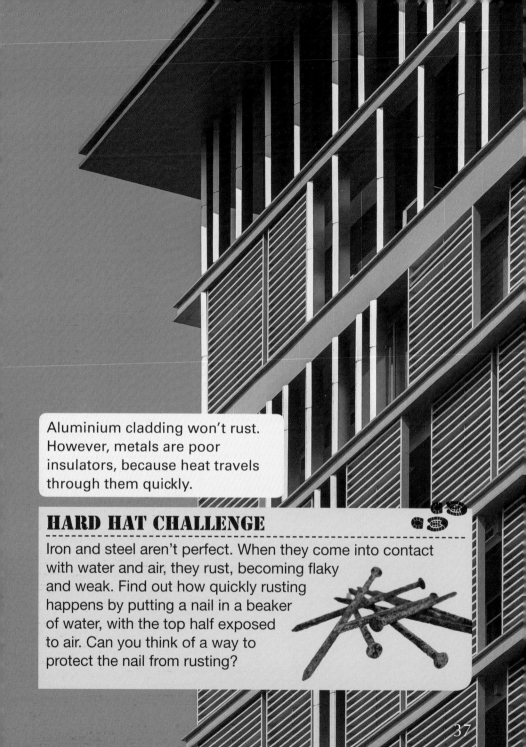

Aluminium cladding won't rust. However, metals are poor insulators, because heat travels through them quickly.

HARD HAT CHALLENGE

Iron and steel aren't perfect. When they come into contact with water and air, they rust, becoming flaky and weak. Find out how quickly rusting happens by putting a nail in a beaker of water, with the top half exposed to air. Can you think of a way to protect the nail from rusting?

Glass

Glass is a feature of homes everywhere from Antarctica to the International Space Station. It's all thanks to one key property – **transparency**.

Roman window glass

Before people learnt how to make flat panes of glass, windows were open holes in the wall. They could be covered with shutters, grids or fabric to keep rain and draughts out, but this made it darker inside.

The large windows of this 16th century mansion made it clear that the owner was super-rich.

At first, large windows had to be made up of many smaller panes.

The Romans were some of the first people to make small windowpanes. They melted sand and mixed it with soda, then poured it into a mould. These sheets of murky blue glass were so expensive to make, they were only used for the homes of very wealthy people. Glass windows remained a luxury for the next 1,600 years.

It wasn't until the 1800s that machines were invented to take over the time-consuming grinding and polishing needed to make flat glass. Glass became cheaper, and larger windows became an option for normal houses too.

If you look through a Georgian or Victorian window today you might spot air bubbles or ripples. It was impossible to make completely flat panes of glass until the middle of the 20th century.

Glass making – and house building – changed forever with the invention of float glass in 1952. **Molten** glass (four times hotter than an oven) is floated on a bath of molten tin, where it spreads out to form a sheet that's almost completely clear and flat.

Today's glassmakers use science to change the properties of glass. Windows can be textured for privacy, toughened to make them shatterproof, or coated to reflect sunlight and keep a house cool.

HOUSE HAZARDS!

Float glass scores ten out of ten for transparency, but like all glass it's fragile. Heavy winds, hailstones and even bird strikes can all damage glass (and birds). However, no other material can do the same job.

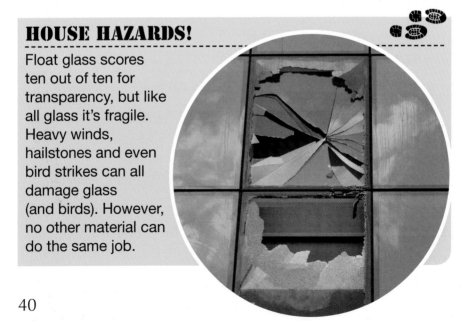

Entire walls can be made from glass, held in place by a strong wooden or metal framework.

Glass walls allow residents to enjoy the view.

Plastic materials

Plastics are remarkable human-made materials. They can be made to mimic the properties of almost any other material, from stone or wood, to metal or glass.

HARD HAT CHALLENGE

Investigate how plastic compares to other materials as an insulator. Put similar sized spoons made of different materials into a mug of hot tap water. Dab a blob of butter or margarine on to the end of each handle. The butter on good insulators will take longer to melt.

waterproof, rustproof plastic
used for pipes and drain pipes

plastic cladding protects
the structural materials

plastic window
frames
and windows

plastic-based foam used for
insulating houses

Plastic can be strong but light,
making it safe to work with.
House builders use plastic
materials in many different ways.

Plastic possibilities

Scientists have created plastics that are as strong as wood, as fireproof as steel, and as good-looking as stone. House builders are experimenting with using plastic to build an entire home.

So why haven't plastic homes replaced wood, brick, steel and concrete? Tradition as well as practicalities shapes our choice of building materials. The materials and building styles that have been used for thousands of years are still in demand.

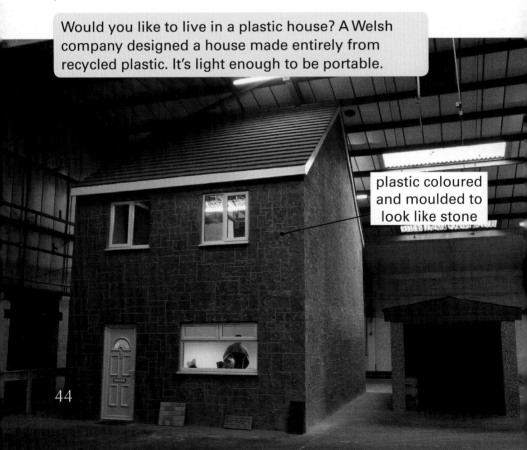

Would you like to live in a plastic house? A Welsh company designed a house made entirely from recycled plastic. It's light enough to be portable.

plastic coloured and moulded to look like stone

A life-sized Lego™ house may sound like a dream home, but after this house was built for a TV show no one wanted to live in it! The tough walls had to be destroyed with chainsaws.

Three-dimensional printing is an exciting new way to build objects from plastic. Dutch architects are experimenting with printing an entire house. There's no waste, because the raw material doesn't have to be cut to shape. Only what's needed is printed. If the owner wanted a new design, the house could be melted down to make a new one!

Sustainable materials

The world's population is growing faster than ever – more than seven billion people need a place to call home. Architects and builders are finding ways to use renewable or recycled materials to build **sustainable** homes.

Walls made from rows of straw bales are held together by pushing wooden posts through the straw.

concrete base

One of the most exciting "new" materials is actually ancient. Straw bale homes are cheap, and keep a house warmer than brick walls. Air trapped inside and between the stalks of straw acts as an insulating coat – it's like living inside a giant puffa™ jacket! Straw bale walls even stand up to earthquakes because straw bales don't crack when shaken.

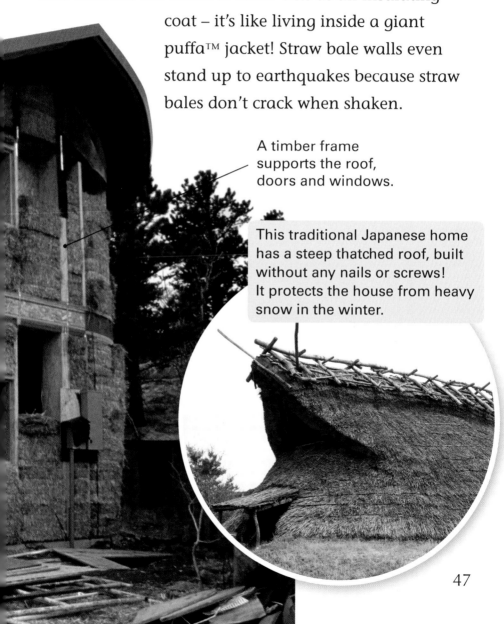

A timber frame supports the roof, doors and windows.

This traditional Japanese home has a steep thatched roof, built without any nails or screws! It protects the house from heavy snow in the winter.

47

Recycled materials

Recycling old materials to build new houses isn't a new idea. Remember the Roman bricks and rubble reused by builders in medieval Europe?

More recently, architects have experimented with reusing everything from packing crates and plastic bottles to old car tyres and aeroplanes. These low-cost ideas are likely to become more popular in the future.

Architects thought like hermit crabs, and turned old shipping containers into new homes.

Wall-to-wall waste

Billions of plastic bottles are dumped in landfill every year, which is a big problem for the planet. Plastic bottles don't **biodegrade**. If bottles are collected and turned into a house, their inability to rot becomes a big advantage.

bottles filled with sand to weigh them down and stuck together with mortar

The walls of this house are made with plastic bottles. Their uniform shape makes them perfect for stacking like bricks.

Building on history

Stone, brick, earth, concrete, glass, metal, straw, plastic, wood ... With so many natural and human-made materials available, how do builders and architects choose how to build a house?

They start by asking themselves questions like these:

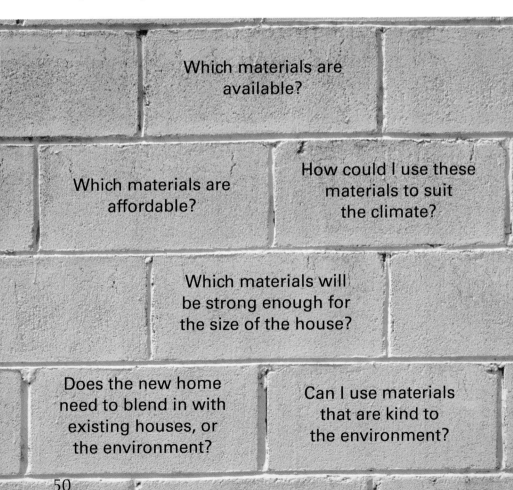

Which materials are available?

Which materials are affordable?

How could I use these materials to suit the climate?

Which materials will be strong enough for the size of the house?

Does the new home need to blend in with existing houses, or the environment?

Can I use materials that are kind to the environment?

House builders around the world continue to come up with innovative answers. Some are finding new ways to use ancient materials. Others are using new materials to enhance traditional home designs.

Y:Cube™ units are made from renewable timber panels. This makes them so light, they can be built in a factory, delivered by lorry, and stacked on site to construct a large building quickly. Special insulation keeps the homes warm without heating.

Glossary

alloys metals made by combining two or more different metals

biodegrade to get broken down by bacteria and fungi

cladding a layer of material added to the walls of a building e.g. to make it waterproof

fired heated to very high temperatures in a special oven called a kiln

Industrial Revolution a period in history when steam powered machines were introduced to factories, producing goods more quickly and on a bigger scale

insulating when a material does not let something pass through it e.g. heat or electricity

lime one of the main ingredients of cement

molten has been melted, so it is liquid

mortar any soft wet material used to bond bricks or stones, that becomes hard (sets) as it dries

organic from living things (or things that were living)

quarried dug

renewable a natural resource that doesn't run out as it is used

shale soft rock that formed from mud or clay

stonemasons people who cut, shape and build with stone

sustainable doesn't run out or damage the planet

tension a stretching force

transparency how see-through a material is

Index

Build your own!

Imagine you are building a house. Think about each part in turn – the foundations, walls, roof, windows, doors and chimney. Which materials would you choose?

Pros   **Cons**

Stone

✔ May be found locally
✔ Can support very heavy loads
✔ Can be extremely weatherproof and long-lasting
✔ Attractive

✗ Difficult to cut, shape and transport
✗ Strong foundations are needed to support heavy walls
✗ Has to be cut to shape, which means waste
✗ May be damaged by earthquakes

Concrete

✔ Does not burn, rot or get eaten by insects
✔ Helps to keep a building warm or cool
✔ Can support a heavy load
✔ Can be used in many different ways
✔ Weatherproof
✔ Can be poured in any shape, cutting down on waste

✗ Can look ugly, so often needs coating
✗ Strong foundations are needed to support heavy walls
✗ May be damaged by earthquakes unless reinforced

Fired bricks

✔ Does not burn, rot or get eaten by insects
✔ Weatherproof
✔ Helps to keep a building warm or cool
✔ Does not need painting
✔ Can support a heavy load

✗ Must be made in a factory, using energy
✗ Expensive to make and transport
✗ Strong foundations are needed to support heavy walls
✗ May be damaged by earthquakes

Pros		Cons

Pros
- ✔ May be found locally
- ✔ May be cheap or free
- ✔ Light and easy to build with
- ✔ Renewable

Wood

Cons
- ✘ May catch fire easily
- ✘ May get eaten by insects
- ✘ May rot in wet weather
- ✘ Has to be cut to shape, which means waste

Pros
- ✔ May be found locally
- ✔ May be cheap or free
- ✔ Easy to make and use
- ✔ Can be used in many different ways
- ✔ Helps to keep a building warm or cool

Earth bricks

Cons
- ✘ Can be damaged by water and heat
- ✘ May be damaged by earthquakes

Pros
- ✔ Transparent
- ✔ Weatherproof
- ✔ Can be made in any shape and size

Glass

Cons
- ✘ Must be made in a factory, using energy
- ✘ Fragile and hard to transport
- ✘ Cannot support a heavy load
- ✘ Not good at trapping heat in or keeping it out

Pros
- ✔ Easy to shape
- ✔ Strong under tension
- ✔ Can be recycled
- ✔ Can support a heavy load
- ✔ Not easily damaged by earthquakes

Metal

Cons
- ✘ Must be prepared in a factory, using energy
- ✘ May corrode (rust) in wet conditions
- ✘ May be damaged by fire
- ✘ Can be expensive

Pros
- ✔ Easy to make in different shapes and colours
- ✔ Can be made with many different properties
- ✔ Waterproof
- ✔ Can often be recycled

Plastic

Cons
- ✘ Must be made in a factory, using energy
- ✘ May be damaged by fire
- ✘ May fade and crack over time (e.g. in bright sunlight)
- ✘ Made using non-renewable resources

Ideas for reading

Written by Clare Dowdall, PhD
Lecturer and Primary Literacy Consultant

Reading objectives:
- make comparisons within and across books
- explore the meaning of words in context
- explain and discuss their understanding of what they have read, including through formal presentations and debates, maintaining a focus on the topic and using notes where necessary
- provide reasoned justifications for their views

Spoken language objectives:
- give well-structured descriptions, explanations and narratives for different purposes

Curriculum links: Science – properties of materials; Design and Technology – plan, make, evaluate

Resources: materials for building shelters; materials for conducting the tests described, pencil and paper, ICT

Build a context for reading
- Ask children to describe where they live (with sensitivity to individual situations), including the materials that their home is made from.
- Look at the front cover and read the title. Discuss the different houses shown, focusing on the materials used to build them. Ask children which one they would most like to live in and why. Read the blurb. Ask children if they can think of places in the world where the listed building materials are used.

Understand and apply reading strategies
- Read pp2–3 to the group. Develop response by focusing on the challenges and questions posed in the text. Lead a discussion about each one, e.g. *what would you use to build a shelter right now, outside?*